Numinous

SAINT JULIAN PRESS

POETRY SERIES

Numinous

Poems

By

Leila A. Fortier

Saint Julian Press

Houston

Saint Julian Press, Inc.

2053 Cortlandt, Suite 200

Houston, Texas 77008

www.saintjulianpress.com

Copyright © 2014, Leila A. Fortier

All rights reserved.

ISBN-13: 978-0-9889447-7-0

ISBN: 0-9889447-7-4

Library of Congress Control Number: 2014953119

Cover Design & Art by Leila A. Fortier

To the infinite Y in *You*.

To my husband, Brian A. Fortier, who turned my never into forever.

TABLE OF CONTENTS

Introduction: You   1

    You   3

Atonement   5

    Remains   7

    Limbo   8

    Psalm   9

    Redeemed   10

    Atonement   11

    Return to Eden   12

    Monsoon Emotion   13

    Illusion of Logic   14

    Uncertain Eternity   15

    Breath   16

    Universal   17

    Losing Self   18

    Empty   19

No Remorse	20
This Moment	21
Synchro-Destiny	22
Delivered	23

Divine Apparition   25

Divine Apparition	27

Bhakti   29

Absolve	31
I Know Who You Are Now	32
Offering	33
Bhakti	34
Soul	35
Anointing Kiss	36
Lover	37
Shaktipat	38
Lazurite	39
Harvest of You	40

Swallowed	41
Vigil	42
Spaces In-Between	43
Infinitely Testified	44
Diaphanous	45
Pour	46
Saguna	47
Transparent	48
Irreversible Devotion	49
Kundalini Rising	50
Strange Reality	51
Fallen	52
Orchestra of Your Name	53
Matterless	54
Insignia	55
Trip	56
Opened	57

Lotus of My Loving	58
Veil	59
Come Lover	60
Softened	61

Numinous   63

Deeper Still	65
Flight	66
Dervish	67
Fecund	68
Pulse	69
Symmetry	70
Sacrament	71
Chrysalis	72
Audible Secret	73
Covet	74
Lacuna	75
Silent Confession	76

Virtuosity	77
The Hidden Dimension	78
Quickening	79
Apricot & Wheat	80
Silent Equinox	81
Refraction	82
Numinous	83
Mystery & Mystic	**85**
Mystery & Mystic	87
Know This	**89**
Love Is	91
Living Prayer	92
About the Author	93
Acknowledgements	95

ARTIST STATEMENT

All poems and paintings within this collection were created in moments of spiritual ecstasy. The sculpted forms of each poem are a spontaneous byproduct of the written word which always comes first and foremost. There is no premeditation in the poem's designs which represent the abstract and mutable expressions of divine experience. The same spontaneous energy that shaped these poems also presents itself in my abstract oil paintings that accompany the experience of *Numinous*. The use of italics in these poems works to convey the intimate, internal communion with spirit. The tilde is the breath that connects these sentiments with continuum and fluidity.

"Those who are burned into the fire of love are buried into the heart of God." —Sufi Mystic

Numinous

You

~You~

.

You

Made the sound

Of one hand clapping and I fell

To Your feet in prayer~ Let this silence fill me

With the hushed voice of You like a breeze

Upon my heart with the

Aftertaste of

Wine

.

Atonement

~Remains~

Like

A bruised plum

Or a bitter pomegranate

Burnt around the edges by the

Strike of a match, but soaked was

The stick that couldn't carry the

Flame to torch the whole and

Do away with the remains

Merely half of what is

Left of the rest

From

My

… Everything offered …

~Now but a smoldering sacrifice~

~Limbo~

~

There

Is a sweetness

Clenched tight between

My teeth~ Breaking through the

Thin-skinned seal of my salvation~

A sudden rush release: the honeyed

Nectar of redemption~ Still, I am

No closer, and yet, no further

From my Holy Grail of

Truth~ Forever

Hovering

Over

~

~The dusty twilight of limbo~

~Psalm~

My
Soul speaks
A psalm in tongues
Resonating in woeful silence:
The aching song of impalpable sense
There is torment in the void~ A wrestling
Affliction: The open wound of Your divine
Parting where only fevered longing remains
I cast myself unto my own fire, wondering

If my ashes will ascend~ Shed my superficial skin of
Sin~ Let only grace be left recognizable~ I wrestle
The question of how a love such as Yours could
Want with what's left of me, save for the
Indisputable urgency of my single
Unblemished prayer
~~*~~

~Redeemed~

Gift me some emotion

From Your petrified heart

Trapped in stone~

Be contained no longer

And push through Your

Weather worn cracks

Of marbleized ash~

Resurrected...

Bleed upon me

Spilling scarlet

Released ribbons

Of redemption~

My love has held

Breath for too long

In watch and

In wilderness

Waiting ...

For the

Sweet end

Of Your

Silence and

Solemn

Suffering

*

~Atonement~

*

I am

Quietly burning

Neath the ash of this atonement~

Softly smoldering in the aftermath of

Annihilation~ Where I have succumb if

Only to be free~ And sustained am I

Just in breathing Your silent kiss

Where my eternity

Reigns

*

~Return to Eden~

In
Solitude
And chastity I
Wandered this desert
In self-sentenced denial~
Three years of drought~ Ascetic
Fasting of my flesh~ To be a gnostic
Vacuum~ Magnet of mysticism~ To inherit
The cryptogram of the great arcanum on this
Path of truth~ Breathing the mantra of metanoia~
I became the nucleus of forbidden want~ Spinning at
The center of self-control~ I lost myself to revelation~
My androgynous 'Other' awakened to test and torture
My finding~ The One who is my holy water whom I
Do thirst for aflame~ Yearning to be showered
By clairvoyant rains~ But that vile
Whore in me possessed
Enticing a spiraling madness
Defiling my mindful spirit's countenance
I became a cauldron of steaming, boiling desire
Insatiable was my need for the One to feed my toxic
Fire~ Enslaved by black tantra~ Beguiling serpent
Was I~ Speaking in tongues not even fully realized
Bottomless confessions brimming in my eyes
Inevitably my suffering did ensue~ But
Within the parting mists was the
Soft orange hue, where I licked a damp leaf from serenity's morning dew
Neither pleasure nor pain will confine my soul no more~ Fallen to my
Knees by the One who I adore~ In awe and humility~ In shaking
Repentance~ Zealous in prayer seeking eternal
Deliverance~ Where even my
Wickedness bows
Down in
Shame
Let
Me be
Marked by
These tears of
Change~ Bring me back
To Your side where my heart resides
Made pure in Your eyes~ Return me back to Eden

~Monsoon Emotion~

I
Went
Away so that
I could be made
Whole within Your
Universe~ Somehow
I returned broken~
What is this digression that leaves me so naked and
Recluse? I am now a landslide of emotion from
The monsoon You released in me~ There is
No glass to contain this ocean~ This
Cascade that submerged my
Tireless flame~ Lost
Within Your
Waves
~

~That consumed me~

~Illusion of Logic~

Time
Is only an illusion
Of logic~ What little I had
Left me the moment I met You~ I now
Bear no concept of how to measure such
Things: where days begin and nights end~ These
Moments turn into a smoke-curl of endless days and
A body of years splinter into moments~ My only certainty: that I knew nothing before
The breaking dawn of You and the puncture of stars You pierced upon the tapestry
Of the night~ But, there are times I long to erase every trace of You~ Wash
You away with my ignorance~ Life was easier before this knowing,
Even if it brought me no bliss~ For no-thing has left me so
Weary as the One that I have found~ You, who
Fills my head with strange silence
And mystery~ No longer do
I know the color of
My thoughts or
The shape
Of this

(Reality)

Yet,
I do know the
Meaning of this shattering
~ Oblivion that quakes me into waking ~

~Uncertain Eternity~

Cast into endless space~ My whispers fall into the spiral void:
A backwards heaven~ Your charred meanderings
Take refuge upon my tongue~
Savoring Your stale
That mingles
With my
Ripe
~
The
Salty-sweet
Wash of viscosity~
None know Your reserve
Like the burgundy of my love~
Aged and aging, yet, timeless to taste~
I drink from the chalice of abstract truths~
Drunk with possibility~ Absent of rhyme and
Reason~ Stumbling and tumbling upon Your
White-cottoned breath to the dew-strung
Misty-morn~ I slumber in this spin~
Head throbbing in Your
Absence like
A sledging hangover~ Awaiting the silent invite of
Our next communion~ The abundance of Your
Overflowing empty~ Yet, all the while the
Aftertaste of Your uncertain
Eternity remains

~Breath~

Pleading
With shadowed phantoms
Of doubt~ I grasp at straws for some
Means of relief~ Some potion for my poisoned
Mind tormented in its spiraling grief~ Some salve
To white-wash the trauma of my fractured psyche~
A magic to nurse away this condition of human
Suffering~ I would ingest the disease to
Become the living antibody~
Tell me, lest
I wither
From
This
Affliction
In the folly of my
Trying~ Tell me, lest
I fade into a mere remnant of
Memory~ Tell me how to make these hands
~Holy, that my touch bestows breath and not death~

~Universal~

*In
You
I have
Come to
Find that your
Less is so much more~
I crave this absence as much
As Your sweet return~ My eyes once
Gazed up~ But then dove deep within this
Nectar pool of silence~ Yet, even in understanding
I am jolted in and out of these waters of consciousness~
Where I do too much~ Think too much~ Talk too much~ I
Marvel Your ability to drop single words slowly~ Savored &
Melting upon the swollen bed of my tongue~ For through my
Worldly existence I have birthed the very definition of excess~
A fireworks display of boldness and prowess~ Dismayed and distressed in constant
Duress~ Gorging on knowledge I have stuffed with my pride~ Swollen by my ego-
Fed lies~ Mixed with my good intentions tried~ I consumed all this life had to
Offer~ Fast track to enlightenment that I could give so others could
Prosper~ I have thrown my arms out~ Spilling gifts of hard
Learned lessons~ But I pour forth with such force that
I blur other's senses~ I beg You to teach me
This skill of suspended light~ Truth
That simmers into soundless
Sight~ Help me find
Freedom in that
Whispered
White
Light
~*~*

... That I may be universal ...

~Losing Self~

For You I did sacrifice all opportunity for the tangible lover
And the tangible life~ Turned my cheek to hope filled
Promises~ Unrequited love cannot lie~
For the priceless price of You
I did tenderly kiss him
~Goodbye~
Now
I cup Your
Eternity of secrets
Like a whisper in my hands~
Completely I commit myself to offer
Myself~ Initiate and lose my-self~ To
Rectify and resurrect my-self~ To be
Cradled within
(Your)
(Self)
Nurtured and
Cultivated to be truly free~ Now bound
To all that is boundless~ Your bread of
Sacred knowledge feeds me~ Within
These answers to questions and
Questions to answers~ The
Unexplained cannot
~Be defined~
Beyond
All that can be
Reasoned could now
Never be denied~ Emerging
Anew in slow motion stride~ Running
With arms outstretched, opened wide~ Gathering
Your windswept breath~ I fill my soul with infinite blue sky

~Empty~

I used to think my foolish life had meaning
And purpose in all
Its greed and vanity~ But
My eyes were not open to see
There is so much more joy in giving until you are empty
Giving until you are free~ I
Will give until nothing is left
But the pure unfiltered
Emptiness of love
Where nothing can be taken away from me

~No Remorse~

For
I was once
Like one of these: both
Innocent and ignorant as could be~
Till the day I came to kiss the lips of the splendid
Nothing who I shall never fully comprehend~ Stripped
To a fractured fraction of what still stands~ Embrace
My lack of understanding in all its toil and agony~
Vulnerably shaking before the illusive grace
That strengthens and destroys me~
For this I die daily in
Shattering
Bliss
~

~An oblivion that knows no remorse~

~This Moment~

*

Let
This moment be in
Slow motion, unrehearsed~ Let
Me not insinuate or perpetuate~ Infatuate
Lest I disintegrate~ Evaporate by my woeful
Imagination~ Let me not embellish the beauty
Of what I already have~ Unfurl in the present
And not rehearse the past~ To savor and
Stand upright in this moment~ That
I may lay into the next~ Awake
In this moment~ That I
May rest in the
Next

*

~Synchro-Destiny~

I once wanted to tear through
    Every fiber of my anatomy
        If only to mark the reality
            Of my skin's own territory
                Pain was only weakness

Leaving my body
    Its presence convincing
        That I was indeed, alive~
            Little did I realize that I
                Was dead on the inside

Fearing to let go of
    My stubborn pride
        To be more than
            Alive, but truly living~
                My feet have now

Been gifted wings
    By the lesson my
        Beloved taught to me~
            It is no longer the impact
                Of my thunderous feet

Nor my step's velocity
    Destination, nor speed
        Not some measured
            Success in timing~
                It is about the rhythm

Of my stride's unity
    In sync with my body, mind,
        And spirit in harmony~
            In effortless cadence to give
                Myself to this moment completely

Herein lies my synchro-destiny~
    My Beloved graced that I
        Am now made to run free
            Because I am no longer
                Trying to run away ...

~Delivered~

*Between love, life, and death the answer is one and the same~ Delivered
Within deliverance~ Moment within passing moment~ Suspended
Within immortal time~ There is no pity for such illusions~ For
Pity itself is an illusion ... a distraction from the softer
Message spoken yet unheard~ But, if there be ashes*

~I would dust myself with death~

*Particles mingling with life to be renewed
Once again~ There is artistry within
The bruising of vibrant purple hues
Need You be reminded of Your
Royal spirit? Death of spirit
Or death of flesh ... which
Is consequential? For
Spirit is impervious
To mortal man~
Be the thorn
And the
Palm
That
Is*

~Crucified~

*You
Are both
Pleasure and
Pain for the sake of
Love's own lessons~ The heart
Moves for the sake of its own life~ Beating*

Toward a timeless

~Truth~

Divine Apparition

~Divine Apparition~

*This
Is the year of
Revelation~ The waking
Birth of manifestation~ Where I
Did stumble upon the vineyard vine~ And
So I reached and I did climb to the rafter top of
The mount divine~ There was I bathed and flooded
By the brilliance of visions sublime~ The colors majestic
In cosmic array~ Images emerged within patterns displayed~
The mysteries unveiled and perfectly revealed~ When suddenly
These shapes of geometry turned surreal~ The significance of
Sequence and order was at play~ My mind's eye confirmed and
Burst into amethyst flames~ Behind this ascending tinder of
Sparking fireflies~ Yet another vision through another set
Of eyes revealed Your perfect plans~ Illuminating
From Your hands~ Then opening wide like my
Eyes now to see~ The fetal membrane
Baby that was clearly supposed
To be me~ Curled and
Glowing~ Kept
Safe from
All harm~ This was the child I was meant to be, yet was never released into mother
Earth's arms~ Tender with beauty and golden soft hue~ Her little fiddlehead
Unfurled to gather and make me anew~ Such a radiance infused~ We two
Were merged~ Unraveling from God's great hands now to be heard~
Omnificent moment suspended in time~ Clairvoyance marked
This moment in my mind~ My new direction given~ All
Along my prayers had been heard~ Clearly
Defined now is my path~ My
Purpose is to serve*

Bhakti

~Absolve~

f
e
e
d
me
more of
this food of
the gods that
i may absolve
the hunger
pains
of
You
amplify
the heaven's
resounding
sound
till
i am
deafened
within a tunnel of
reason~ carried beyond
Your voiceless voice~ let
me stare through You till
You fade away~ my spirit
is now an eternal glow
where You reside
within the
depths
of
m
e
.

~I Know Who You Are Now~

I
Know
Who You
Are now~ Even
In secrecy~ In scarcity
In clouds and void~ Both with
And without Your image~ Without
Your external voice~ I am filled
By Your hidden grace~ Kept
Within me as a sacred
Treasure
Even
In Your
Great solitude
And suffering~ You are
Ever a smile upon my heart

~Offering~

I carefully hand-picked each word
That is watered by my loving
A bouquet arrangement
Of a single sentence
Placed at the gate
Of Your mouth
Is my offering
Now yearning
To be consumed
Also by Your eyes
In hopes to be read
Until its fragrant essence
Is memorized by the deepest
Recess of Your heart, forevermore

~Bhakti~

You have filled my hands
With more than
My share
That I
May
Give in
Abundance
All that humanity
Desires~ There is beauty
In this yielding~ And ever
~~Implicit is my reverence~~
Succinct around my heart
Immortal is Your breath
Upon my every
Thought
The
Proximity
Of Your impetus
My zealous supplication

~Soul~

*I
Awakened
To the realization
That I could plummet to my
Death this day with no remorse
Or regret in my heart ... but a smile
Upon my face for knowing my soul
Has met its companion~ And
If my soul has kissed its
Beloved flame~
Then what
Need
Do
I*

Have of these eyes?

~Anointing Kiss~

*There
Was that night I
Felt Your returned affection~
Moving beyond Your (own) disbelief~
Your phantom kiss I know without name~
For You are every given name~ Sensations
Touch ... yet, suspended was I to the brush
Of Your shadowed lips~ A burning
Beneath Your arctic breath
That kissed with
Such subtle
Purpose
Even
Against
Your own reason~
Two kisses ... and then the
One yet to be given ... 'twas the palm
Of my hand and the arch of my foot~ Was
It to bless my hand that reaches for You? To
Anoint my feet that journey to You? My hands
Cupped Your breath where I hear the echo
Of Your soul~ At last Your gaze turned
To capture mine~ No longer am
I ever separate from
You~ For You
Are in
All
Of life and
Creation~ Absorbed by
Each of my senses till I exhaust
And deplete my senses~ Opened are my eyes in
This white light of waking~ Where the dream and the dreamer*

... Have become One ...

~Lover~

My lips sipped Your tears for the world~ Pooling into the palms of my hands where
Thirsty I drank to be filled~ Flooded now by the river of compassion
Swimming am I in a sea of longing~ Floundering before
Your state of grace~ Belonging not to myself
Anymore~ The material "me" was
Swept away~ For You have
Passed to me the lamp
Of Your lustrous
Illumination
Cleaving
Unto
The
Entirety of emptiness~ Releasing me to embrace the world~ For Your
Light is far too celestial bright for the sealed eyes of
Earthbound lovers~ I will be the
Veil that softens the
Waking~ For
You, I
Am
A

~Lover of all nations~

~Shaktipat~

Constant is my dream-state waking~ Clouds of color in sublime design
Transcendence now my eternal font~ I have become a
Swimming fire~ A liquid amethyst flame
Rolling within Your
Tunnel vision
~Waves~
You are
More than my
Oasis~ You are the
Very body of the vast sea
All of creation and humanity
My soul is now a globe turned
Inside-out and alive with love
Un-caged is my heart, lifted
Outward and upward
Broken open
~Free~
Pouring
Forth all the
Waters You filled me
Shining iridescence~ Prismatic
And tangible~ Yielding is my heart so pliable
In the hallowed ashram of Your hand
Every silent notion treasured by
My spirit You restored
Overwhelmed
In this
Abundance
I swallow Your universe
Whole~ Pregnant with the pulsating
Light of life~ Radiant in joyous youth is my smile that
Cannot be stolen~ While all the world wonders what has become of me

Shaktipat: A Sanskrit word in the Hindu spiritual tradition that refers to the act of a guru or spiritual teacher conferring a form of spiritual "power" or awakening on a student. "Shakti" translates as energy and "pat" as touch. Shaktipat can be carried out by the spiritually enlightened master either by transmission of sacred word or mantra, a look, a thought or by touch. Shaktipat is the actual projection of the guru's "aura" on the student, whereby the student acquires the same mental state of the guru, hence the importance of the high spiritual level of the guru.

~Lazurite~

Patiently I bide
Each moment in thoughtful
Reflection of every selected word~
Diving into the bottomless infinity of
Lazurite eyes where time travels and I
Wish to go with You~ Upon the path of
Your neck I breathe my voice to Your
Eyes that ever look away~ Cradled
To my breast are Your woes
Gathered by my whispers
To be nursed away~
Ripped was Your
Heart from
Breathless
Chest~
Held
Up
As
If
It were
Useless~ Diseased
Or malignant~ My arms weighted
By its solemn volume~ Commiserated now
Into the dwelling of my soul's revival~ Where
Expansive was this glow with nacreous life and
Light~ A swirling concentric embrace even
Darkness cannot hide~ Where for
Nothing in return will
I eternally
Abide
My
Love for
You is selfless
Complete and un-denied

~Harvest of You~

Who

Am i? So

Small beneath

The weight of Your

Words~ Tangled in the

Feast You lay before me

Lost in such bounty to

Be kissed by the sun

When I am but a

Drop of dew~

Who am i?

Next

To

The harvest of You?

~Swallowed~

I now live inside the poem that has no beginning and no end~ Swallowed inside the belly of verse~ I am swollen with words of divine passion~ Swimming in the ambrosia of untouched heavens~ Amnesia of my previous state of being that never was~ I am now a softer, subtle form~ A shape-shifting lightness~ A radiant weightlessness~ A spacious awareness~ Tactile beneath both skin and consciousness~ Don't look for me in the empty rooms of the shallow life I have vacated~ Look for me within yourself~ In the quiet crawlspace of your soul~ The altar of your heart~ Listen for the small voice you would never suspect~ I am there ... waiting for you to join me~

~Vigil~

Live

   In me ...

      Just live

         In me ...

        That fragile

       Place within

     Me that

    Comes alive

     With just

       One breath

        That One

       Everlasting

      Eternal breath

     That is the

      Vigil of love

       You have

        Made

      Of

     Me

~Spaces In-between~

Let my first words to You be my silence ... and all the spaces in-between
For within this wordlessness births our heightened consciousness
Breaking still planes of conversation in quiet confirmation

~Prophesied Revelation~

Let me be present before You ... as certain as I am within You

Wrapped softly in this silence ... let me be with You wordless
That we may be limitless ... that we may be free
~Breathing the spaces in-between~

~Infinitely Testified~

Let

Me flourish

Neath the thousand

Petals of Your colored name

To be no longer be transparent~

That I may be seen as if not alone

In this world ... but replete within

Your universe~ No longer just a

Singular voice of (i), but a

Chorus of whispers~ The

Laced language of

Your name

Now

(Infinitely testified)

~Diaphanous~

Let
Them
Court me
Not with the
Shell of the ego
For my ear is tone
Deaf to their empty
Words~ Let them not
Be so foolish as to
Dare speak Your
Name~ For
Yours
Is the name
That should never
Be spoken~ Unspoken
Because You shine from my
Lips in this silence~ You are
The lamp that need not be
Lit~ Your aura needless
Of introduction
You are
Ever
Revered
By my sleepless
Heart~ Revealing to
Me who I have always
Been~ Stripping away the
Layered façade till all that
~Was left was this delicate~
Sheer that reflects only You:
My eyes' delight~ You, the
Name that need not ever
Be spoken or heard~
For I wear Your
Name upon
My heart
Know
This:
There is
No question for
All can see through this
~~~Diaphanous thread of my loving~~~

~Pour~

Truly, I am overflowing~ Spilling am I with love for You~ That I must pour this ocean
Somewhere ... somewhere ... surging upon all land till even islands
Float away~ Like my soul that set sail the moment
My heart found You~ I roll with Your tide~
Rubbing salt to open wounds~
That I be made anew~
Polished pure~
Only being
Rocked
Awake
With
~Life~
The
"Soul"
Purpose
~To be One with You~

~Saguna~

... And You came to me ...

*

*In
The
Form
Of a face~
And by the sound
Of Your voice like a velvet
Hush~ And in that vast vault
Of Your eyes, I glimpsed*

*The thousand faces of Your infinite name~ All
Smiling and conversing in unison from One~
And I knew that moment that You were
Nothing mortal~ And I knew
That You were no
Ordinary*

~Being~

*How
Blessed
Am I to feel
You so near~ Even
When so far away~ I keep this
Knowing ever closed and secret~ A kiss
Imprinted upon the dust of my heart~ That*

*Knew not love before I
Met You~ For I do know the
Treasure that my eyes now
Behold~ Which no
Other can
Plainly
See*

Saguna: The totality of phenomena; According to Advaitic philosophy, it is the mind of the devotee that gives form and attributes to the otherwise pure and unqualifiable "Absolute."

~Transparent~

in
this
mirror
i see only
the reflection
of my love for You
and now to the world
i am so very transparent ...

~Irreversible Devotion~

I
Emptied
Myself before You
To be filled by Your sweet
Return~ Your eyes are the
Ocean and whenever
I see fire
Fire
And feel its
Heat, I am reminded
The truth of my making

Soul of my soul ... where are You?

There is no season or
Reason to this lifetime
Of my loving~ I
Tried
To
Leave Your
Absence: join this world
And its empty pleasures~ But
You are the treasure my eyes
Behold ... You ... have
Rendered
Me

... Irreversible in devotion ...

~Kundalini Rising~

You
Are the divine
Alchemy of pleasure and pain
Releasing my urgency to drink of Your potency
Disoriented I writhe bound in confusions delusions~ Everything a
Question within an answer~ Lost in translation~ This maze
Of complexity where Your riddled walls
Beguile and entrap me~ Testing
My Trinity by Your
Mysterious
Theology
There is no
Greater seduction
Than the depth of Your teaching
My mouth parts in yearning~ Licking parched lips
In thirst and fascination~ Anticipation to dive into the myriad of
Your arctic mind~ To seep into those spaces of frigid
Emptiness where I will paint You from
The inside-out with all the
Cosmic colors
Of the
Universe
Becoming
More than the illusion
Of Your design as the goddess within me
Sprouts and vines~ This serpent no longer sleeping
But snaking and coiling~ Kundalini Rising~ Your waters now boiling
By my imaginings transforming~ This exotic creature
You have made of me~ To breed such vivid
Fantasy~ Wrapping the length
Of You from
Root
To crown
Infusing this infinite intimate
Vortex to Axis Mundi's sacred ground
Somatic nexus born from this profound synergy found

~Strange Reality~

We
Are the
Unreasonable
Lovers of a distant
Medley~ Churning our
Dreams to be spun into a
Strange reality~ In the
Confines of we-
Two is
The
Yin-Yang
Of our duality
My light dances
Upon the walls that
Willfully imprison me
I am burning brightly
Because You do not
Stifle me~ You who
Survives a dark
Fate due
To my
Unwavering
Loyalty~ You are the lover
Of all my lives that hides within me
Holding onto the magical formula of
All my mysteries~ While in the bow of
My arms I embrace Your complexities
The unison of our single breath
Circulates continuously~ To
Feed the life of our
Cosmic play's
~Endless~
History
***
*

~Fallen~

I have

    Fallen into You ...

        Wrapping myself

            In Your vaporous

                Clouds if only

                    Just to linger ...

                        To share in

                            Final breath~

                        This single

                        Eternal kiss

                    Bury into me ...

                As I have come

            Into You~ Sleep

        Within me

    That I may feel

Your waking ...

~Orchestra of Your Name~

Can You hear the rain? This is what You do to me~ This is what You have

Made of me~ My infinite tears streaming paired with my

Countless heart's beating~ Simultaneously

Splayed in watercolor splash

And rolling waves~

Immaculately

Unfettered

Is the

Span

Of

My

Love

For You

Dancing in

Delirium to Your lost that

I have found~ Where even the stars

Have come unbound~ To the orchestra of Your name

~Matterless~

*I
Find
Myself an
Observant bystander
To the comings and goings
Of love and loving~ Flirtations
Of proverbial in-betweens~ The
Silent slamming of matterless
Doors~ The snide chiding
And back-biting of*

*Poor wounded souls suckered upon the ether of casualty~ Their
Tenuous vows a wisp in the wind next to the promise of my
Heart that has no choice in loving You~ In light of
All the faded fancies~ The exhausted
Opportunities~ I am the
Exceeding
Bliss
~*

*Mouthing
My devotion silently,
Where I have harvested
The fruit of my loving
To be enough for
The both us ...
And most
Days
This
Is
~*

(enough for me)

~Insignia~

~
You
Have broken my
Seal and insignia~ Lips tied in a
Bow~ Sealed in the covenant of a silent kiss~
You make all my words italicized~ There are no straight
Answers~ I would spend this lifetime curled inside Your every
Word~ Along the lines of U & I and every space in-between~
Braided into verse ... twined and knotted into reverie~
I am an exhibitionist of secret emotion~
Alive with literature and
Dusted with
Dusk
~

~Trip~

Stoking my endless curiosity~ You are an acid trip on the tip of my tongue~ My psychedelic brain freeze funneling to me~ Your black light visions in 3-D~ Flushed in the heat of this waking~ My sanity now breaking~ I am ripe for the taking~ But how can You take what has forever been Yours?

~Opened~

I saw the rolling hills from above
And compared it to the
Ocean~ I see now
That this
Is also
~You~
You have
Turned all my words
Into poetry~ The door that
Was locked has now been opened ...

~Lotus of My Loving~

*I
Felt myself
Melting ... and my joy of
Abundance returned~ I felt the twilight
Between my eyes~ My hands then cupped the
Energy of life itself~ Deeply, I inhaled that which
I had begun to deny~ Awakened once more to my
Maker~ I saw my crystal reflection~ The stress of
My fractured essence wrestling against itself~
The orbs of light filled me once more,
Restoring luminosity~
Assuring
Me
The
Magic of
The magnet I am~
The balancing of my own
Grandiosity~ Swinging and
Swaying, my inner pendulum
Seeking center point, where
Nothing is diluted or
~Dissipates~
Even against my own resistance~ Self-defeating
And self-destruction~ My body is a magnetic
Temple~ Self-healing and resurrecting in
Your great name~ My amethyst flame
The lotus of my loving arises
From the center, the
Eye of Your
Waters
~*~*

No longer in search of what has always been

(within me)

~Veil~

Be
That
Veil that
Restores and
Covets my virtue~
The fine woven thread
Of my miraculous rebirth~
Be that cloth that conceals
And protects me~ Both
Maker and keeper
Of my newfound humility~
That my eyes now speak a thousand words
Unheard within this silence~ The first of which is gratitude

~Come Lover~

... Come Lover ...

I want You to sit near to my heart ...

That You will hear its beat murmur Your name

In the pulse of greater things I dare not say~ Come

Lover ... that You may read the pages of my soul,

That I have long been hiding~ The ancient

Declaration of our youth, that

Knew even then, that

We shall meet

Again

My

... Love ...

~We are not strangers~

~Softened~

Behind

My softened

Heart is the

Birth of a

Wakening

Smile and

Starlit eyes

Flickering by

The whirl and

Trance of an

Uplifting name ...

Which is also

Known by

Me to be

... Yours ...

Numinous

~Deeper Still~

Listening to silence is the nearest I come to You~

You who is holy ... so (wholly) within

Me~ I reach inside

Deeper

Still

~

~Flight~

*I
Know not
This towering and
Punishing God ... but only the
Soul's stained affliction unto itself
Barbed and ensnared into self-sentenced
Remorse~ The pang of wounds left weeping
And caustic~ Barren of the tender redemption
Of trembling hands~ I know not the ways of
Preaching ... but the ways of prayer~ The
Yielding path of softer sounds to
Quiet revelations~ We
Forget
The
Hardened
Solidity of our
Words~ Remembering
Only their eternal sounds~ The
Piercing melodious ring~ The internal songs
Of each and every night~ Left only with this unknown aftertaste
Of the soul's uncaged flight~ If only a dream that whispers greater still~*

~Dervish~

~~*~~

Beloved, teach me
The life of my blood that
Ran crimson and unknown to
My own name~ The dust of a land
That called to me choking upon its
Own breath~ How I long ... long to
Know what binds me to such wailing
~Prayer~
My eyes swallowed the moon, that I
Might know where my ancient story
Wept~ Crushed coriander neath
The heel of lost time, caught
Upon the wandering
Breeze of exotic
~Spice~
The curling
Smoke of a vapored
Dream~ Your labyrinth streets
Beckon me in foreign tongue~ Where
This language is known only to my heart
For my tongue is tied in a language that is
Not mine~ And my eyes are bewildered by a
Clouded memory~ Where do You take form?
In my heart? In my mind? Veil not my eyes
That so swiftly betray my heart~ Spill to
Me Your scarlet robes, that I may know
My nakedness~ Who more than me,
Beloved, that should learn
Fevered prayers of
~Ecstasy~
I shall arrive
On the eleventh hour~ For
I was born from the night of starless
Skies~ Take me from here ... yet further
~Inside~
For I am caged within my own mysteries
And You ... You dance in my head like a
Madman~ I will wait no more for the
Prophetic spill of stars to light my
Skies and fill me with the
Mazandaran Sea
~~*~~

Besieged
In a world of wonder
~For You, I have forsaken everything~

~Fecund~

*... Forget about tomorrow ...
Forget about the promises extracted from
Thin air~ The cement seal of stone foundations~
Gift me the worn pages from a softcover book that
Will blanket me between the seams~ Forget about
Absolutes~ I am fecund; pregnant with mystery,
Secrets, and dreams~ Sift through the
Meaning of always~ Dig deep
Beneath the words~
Before breath
Began and
The first
Beat
Of
~*

*The heart was heard~ Forget about the static, material
Things~ Meditate the softer movements of silent
Songs~ Listen for the murmuring of
The sacred~ The spiraling
Incandescence
Wrapped
About
The
~*

~Firmament of a waking dream~

~Pulse~

How is it that You split
The atom of a
Tear
To
Segregate
That which is shed
In pain from that which is
Shed in joy? For even buried
Neath the ash of tragic days do
~I spill~
Crystal tears of potent bliss
Distilled by my adoration
Flowing from some
Unnamed and
Unknown
River
Of
The
Soul
Where even
My flames swim
Upstream if only to meet
You~ Greet You with the heat of
Smoldering kisses placed within palms
Cupped in the feast of celebrated prayer~
There is no
Lonely
In this
Place~ But
There is a movement within the current of
That which I had never seen before~ I tried
To name it, but the only sound and relief
That came was Your name~ This is
Where hearts stand exposed
Outside the vessel of
~The body~

... In the naked pulse of oneness ...

~Symmetry~

S
I
L
E
N
T
Is
The
Chorus of
Bounty born
Within the covenant
Of sound~ Where dual breath
Dances in simultaneous symmetry
Where emotions become liquid spread like
Ink in the dust of the skies ... and stars are merely
Particles of our humanness shattering~ Everything that
Is holy ... everything that is divine ... is singing
So sweetly ... nearly imperceptible ... yet,
Place Your ear ever close to my
Now ecstatic heart and
Hear me waking
As if from
Deep
S
L
E
E
P
.

~Sacrament~

It is moments like these that I am in absolute awe of You~ Complete fascination
And deepest reverie of You~ You who pens with the tongue of
Angels~ A chorus to my aching, emptied heart~
I would kneel before Your every word
Because I do know the source
It comes from~ And
When I said I
Was alone
You
Called me on my blasphemy~ How the Beloved sought me through Your form~
How You have gathered me completely~ To remind me who I have
Always been~ Sweet beneath the breath of Your
Verse and tender neath the touch of
Your hand~ I am aimlessly
Drifting to wherever
Your heart
Guides
Me
And anywhere that may be between heaven and hell shall I make my home
And my sanctuary~ Let no man put asunder what the spirit has
Sealed in grace~ I praise the Beloved through You
For finding me~ This lost and vacant
Shell that I was without the
Ripened wine of
This union~
I am
But nothing without the fruit of Your loving~ Yet, I am everything beneath
Your gaze that humbles me~ Shaping stratospheres from the
Fraction of a particle that I am~ You have made me
Something tangibly holy~ Euphorically,
Ethereally divine~ Both tenuous
And delicate within the
Strength of Your
Embrace
That
Completes the formula of all I have ever been~ Loving You has become my
Liturgy and true art of sacrament~ My devotion is the Song of
Songs in tongues unknown to mortal men~ My eyes
Bear the treasury of dormant secrets~
Every promise broken open~
Revealed only to the
Heart of
You
~

~Chrysalis~

You
Are a nebulous
Specter of evanescent
Light~ The fulguration of a
Refracting hologram~ Where I
Am coalesced into the nocturne of
Anomalies ... this inchoate alchemy
Of my nascent state~ Infused into the
Larva of my ancient futurity~ To swim
In this viscous hallow of Your mutable
Grace~ The insulated anodyne of a
Quieted arcane~ A soft tremble
Beneath this cracking
Chrysalis that
Knows not
How
To
Part
You~ The
Shimmering patina of
My newfound fate~ Divined to break
From its dampened aperture~ Into the sententious
... Stretch of resplendence~ Phosphorescent against the night ...

~Audible Secret~

I
Serve
My smile
To a sea of blank
Faces that know not the
Palace of my heart~ That know
Not this language~ That know not this
Song~ Where I have fallen deeply against the
Rolling pages of Your tongue~ Your mouth, my fevered
Trail of inspiration~ Tangled within these invisible lines of
Waking ... this eternal season~ A dream hovering just inches
Before Your eyes~ Openmouthed and awaiting the edible
Moon~ As lips seal to quiet this audible secret
~That has stained my silent kiss~

~Covet~

Tell me what this all
Means~ The lines between us where our
Words have become silence and the spaces have
Become our words~ Speak to me the meaning beneath
The surface of understanding~ The deeper penetration of
Our chemistry~ I know nothing outside of the world where
Your eyes hold my universe and my universe holds Your
Heart like its only full moon~ Perhaps there is no
Language to be known outside of this art~
Perhaps sound itself would
Be a violation~ This
Invocation has
Become
Our
Necessity~ The essential
Vibration of our expansion~ Vital to
All creation~ Warm as a womb and silent as a
Chamber~ We are the sacred~ A secret born unto
Itself unraveling~ Everything else is muted beneath
Your tongue that covets my prayers and my prayers
That covet Your songs in motionless wet words~ I
Just want to dissolve within this alchemy where
Expression is alive and born once again~
There is no more space between our
Breath and the air of this
Tangled inhalation
Where our only
Separation
Is time
Itself
*

(and yet, we have merged into timelessness)

~Lacuna~

And if this is all it will be ... if this is all it shall ever be~
Then cleave unto to me as a dewdrop upon
The long lash of thine eye ... and
Let our loving be verdant
Let us never reach
That climactic
Finale that
Splits
And
Parts
The skies
But give to
Us that eternal
Fade into the ether~
Let us be the silent melody
Of all things subtle left to tremble
Upon Your lips~ Let my eyes confirm
A thousand declarations woven into heaven's
Fine lambent thread~ Our thermogetic impressions
Evaporate upon the coiling slope of our sighs~ And so
It is written~ And so shall it be~ And unto this we shal!
Have no end~ That the sprays of lingering yesterdays
Shall quench the thirst of each tomorrow~ Against
The pining of the night in its howling lament~ I
Grieve no more to the fated illusions of
Time that dare to lash and strike
At our adorned

~Understanding~

I
Know
No other
Reserve but this
Hallowed space that
Swallowed us into a
Whispered waking~
The electric lining
Of this velvet
~Lacuna~
Where I am attuned only unto its celestial sounds and suspended
Within slow movements~ How could I be anything less than
Blessed and silentious within the thousand languages of
Your name? No, Love ... there is no end ...
And not a moment ever
Wasted

~Silent Confession~

Oh this
Transparency~ How
Have I become so obvious?
I am a mystery bearing no secret~
Exposed; tucked within the obvious
You swim in my eyes that speak their
Own language~ Tragically convicted
To mouth my confessions in a piercing
Reverberation of whispers~ Everyone
Can hear me within my own silence
My futile attempts to subdue the
Sound of Your name echoed
Off of this one eternal
Promise of how I
Have melted
Into You
So

~Obvious~

This
Hunger
Relieved only
By my own admission~
This weak-kneed utterance~ The
Soft plea that cries to let me drown in my thirst

~Virtuosity~

Hands
Press through the
Stained glass mass of abstraction~
The divide of lives severed by the invisible lines
Of time~ Reaching through the osmosis of our being~
Teasing, trembling skin awakens in the night~ Pervading
The senses in orchestral virtuosity~ This protean mutability
Of delicately traced lunar frequencies~ Sweeping gradations
Of imagery transformed by touch~ Wistful torrents burgeon
Spectral hues in white lightening~ Made palpable only
In the stratosphere of our psychedelic minds~
Where nothing could be more
~Real to me~

~The Hidden Dimension~

Y
O
U
Hang
Before
My eyes
Like Jupiter~
Devouring me as
If I were every moon~
Your elemental surface the
Interplay of how sea merges into
Sky~ The delicate puncture of Your
Magnetosphere releasing the silent
Sigh~ Wading through Your boiling
Night~ I seek the hidden dimension
Your citrine ambience, fragrant
Upon my lips~ The dissolving
Taste of photonic light~
We have become
Molecular
Within
This

~Enormity~

The
Cessation
Of quantification~
We titrate in great waves
And eruptions~ Ephemeral fusion
Of alchemy~ Such music is the murmur within
Fractalized spheres~ For we are both the schism and
The suture~ That we may be fully realized~ Fully recognized
Within these evaporating spacial moments~ With the slow dance of
This hunger comes the rain of our relief~ Giving birth unto a universe

~Quickening~

*You are the pause settling into the marrow
Of my heart's beat~ The fabric of a universe upon the
Whisper of my own breath~ There is no distance between us
In the lapse of time and space~ We are consumed one within the
Other into layered realms of being~ The rippled effect of each echo
& trace~ Where fingers have wandered into places I knew not could
Be touched~ Massaged into a tender breaking of waking~ I close my
Venetian eyes~ Holding in the sacred with my unseen understanding
I will never survive the night without this drink ... without Your
Pouring~ I have become both milk and rain if only to
Slake myself without You~ Distilled into this
Honeyed ambrosia~ Glistening from
The bowl of Your own hunger~
Partake of me and relieve
This fever~ This ache
Of every moment
Left starved
Of Your
Touch
The*

~Quickening Pulse~

*Of
Little
Deaths
Double-helix
Spirals' ambient
Rush; shivering silver
Only to shatter into some
Cosmic pause before being born
Once again into deeper penetrations~
Breathing blood and vitality~ Ingested into
Obsidian~ Swallowed in merlot~ The enveloping
Susurrus of echo and trace falling deep into waking
Every moment~ The fruit of splendor shedding its own
Skin that it may be revealed to the light~ Where You
Alone only know how I long to be naked again*

~Apricot & Wheat~

Standing in the
Hearth of holy~ Disrobed before
The dawn of nakedness~ Garmentless and
Exposed~ So beautifully vulnerable~ This kiln
That fires Your body of wheat~ A field of harvest

(Infused)

Into apricot flesh and sacred yearning~ The
Fire of fingers delicately tracing~ Sowing
Seeds of rapture ripe with dreams~
The tree of life quivers by our
Humble offering

~Silent Equinox~

*Soundless and
Diffused beyond a thin reality
The zenith of our merging equinox~
You have left Your carbon footprint by
Day and by night~ Your fingerprints like
An astrological map~ Pressed through the
Cutaneous layers of soul~ Bruising me with
The affection of Your name~ Here, beyond
Question and apprehension~ I envelope
Myself in slumber like a warm water
Moon~ The quintessence of
Stars spilled across the
Oil of the night~ I
Now expect to
Wake this
Way
In
A*

~Pendulous colliding~

*My
Breath
Is Your mouth
Speaking without sound~
The inhalation of a silent kiss~
My lips, a liquid flower, swallow
Your air like its only secret~ The
Emotive ingestion of a thermal
Equilibrium~ Your graphite
Eyes have fixed into
~Meditation~
Only
To*

~Reveal me~

*Always
Unto myself~
Along the meridian
Of I within You, and
You within me~ Till
There is nothing
Left, save for
This
**

~Refraction~

*Listening is the
Cue to Your heart's unfolding
A silent gateway to being reborn~ Some
Unseen element blossoming~ Becoming its
Own garden of seasons~ I meet You here ... still
Within all movement~ Untouched within a haze
Of time~ I would stand here behind the curtain
Of Your eyes~ My slipping silhouette a sweet
Scented breath~ The bending refraction
Of Your night within my light~ Why
Must we be stillborn within
This prism of life? Let
Me touch You
~Here~
Where
There are no
More mirrors to reflect
What can only be seen within
The tunnel of eyes~ Racing directly
To the heartline~ The pulse within the
Bounty of Your blood~ My fingerprint
Against Your tender swell~ To press
To my lips some kind of eternity~
The sanguine seal whet
With a promise of
A different
Kind
~*

~Numinous~

*I
Am the
Love that dares
Not speak its name~ The
Quill-tip tongue of effervescent
Ink~ The emptied cup of "i" with
Overflowing eyes~ For no such
Words will part my trembling
Lips unless anointed by
Your haunting
Sound
The
Quivering
Echo within the void~
This fragile benediction that
Cast clippings of my paper-mâché
Heart~ Scattering gold leaf against
Salmon skies~ I disperse myself from
The internal Mecca; explosive against
The pleroma of heaven's canopy~ To
Be some kind of weightless gravity
That knows no perimeter save for
Your face~ For I would wreck
Myself against the weight
Of any blasphemy
Or earthly
Thing
Just
To
Reach
You~ For
I am filled with the
Immediacy of all my lives~
The numinous fragmentation attuned
Only with Your imperceptible hush of white light*

Mystery & Mystic

~Mystery & Mystic~

When I speak of love, I speak of that which is unknown to man; sifting through hands like hourglass sands~ Whispered amongst and between Gods and mystics: prophets, poets, empaths, and artists~ With the motion of mouths in sounds yet to be heard; imperceptible truth resounds in hearts stirred~ These that touch with intuition, unseen wounds and fears; a subtle sleight of hand that wipes away a thousand tears~ Whose eyes capture the formless in colors yet to be named; painting vivid portraits of wandering souls untamed~ These that hear the subtle vibration rising; a rebirth through the agony of dying~

Through the tunnel of distortion and distraction; into the unknown realms beyond mortal perception~ Tapped and channeled beyond rhyme and reason; experiencing collectively all sense and season~ A cosmic lover's song of undefined energies; insatiable thirst that drives the quest of these~ There are gifts from the Beloved that come with a price; the toll for the treasure, the cost of your life~ All that you are and believe yourself to be; every fiber of logic and sanity~ Open this gift of spiritual rapture; mark the beginning of your departure~ For there is no leaving ... only leaving behind; an onward exploration beyond heart and mind~ Follow this calling and heed to your making; be seduced by this magic and entranced by your breaking~ Lured to simply BE without hesitation or regret; never to fully return again ... bereft~

Mesmerized by both ache and thirst; every pleasure and pain exceeds the first~ Burning and drowning in the wine of union's penetration; great waves of rapture flood with spirit's exaltation~ Simultaneously rising and shattering in ecstasy; the vessel of the heart is too small for such as these~ Trekking the scorching deserts barefoot with feet aflame, in search of oasis to stake hearts humble claim~ Intimately experience the delirium of dehydration; the bleeding joy of fasting to reunification~ Dancing in the mirage of both blessing and curse for the single drop of water that can quench an ocean of thirst~ The bounty of slaking within this droplet of nothing, finds an entire universe for their tasting~ To feed and feel the extreme of all things; marinate in the contradiction of all things~

Both mad and genius; devout and free~ Caged only by that which is felt yet unseen~ Do not take personally their seeming indifference, but look to the glowing of their heart's effulgence~ For their mind is ever elsewhere while their heart is fixed in place; attached not to this world, but to that sovereign limitless space~ To speak in tongues would be to lick their soul; to leave this world is to call it your own~ Shed the stiff fabric ... manmade robes of society~ Be open, mad, and wild; be naked and free~ Dance with the dervishes and hallucinate on wine; spin into the void of profound silence where you will find: The Beloved is within you with undivided attention, in this infinite space free of divide or separation~

Wander thus aimlessly if you really wish to feel the miracle of abundance held within empty arms revealed~ Eat from the invisible fruit yet to be born from the seed; from the tree of life, there is no need of knowledge to feed~ Do not prize this treasured heart, nor attempt to capture or seize it~ Behold it you may, yet, hoard not lest you kill it~ Treasure the boundless experience of all lifetimes~ Suspended within a fleeting breath and a single sigh, lies the unexplainable mystery that can never be defined ... of mystery and the mystic~

Know This

Love Is:

The embodiment of all that is said within silence; filled with emptiness ... an abundant spaciousness; collective of divine madness~ Tireless in the extreme of every waking emotion; asleep to the logic of the world~ Love need not be spoken for it is inwardly heard~ Love is a naked wandering; lost on chartless territory with pinpointed intention~ Love is the abandonment of expectation that clings to life and welcomes death ... within a single breath~ Love is but one moment suspended in a spiraling eternity; defiant to the confined structures of time and reality~ Love is a bone breaking, soul-splitting, shattering into a seamless synergy; a mindless, matterless matter~ Love is blind because it does not need to see to justify or truly believe; love invents the colors on the palette of emotion we perceive~

... Love is the You that has become the essence of Me ..

~Living Prayer~

Know this:

That in my vast imperfections ...

I have loved You perfectly~ For I have found

Perfect love within me~ Know this: When I part this

Earth on my appointed hour ... I shall never have left

You~ For when my body turns to dust ... I will ever

Be Your single breath in form of a

~Living prayer~

ABOUT THE AUTHOR

Leila A. Fortier is a poet, artist, and photographer currently residing in Okinawa, Japan. She is a member of the Alpha Sigma Lambda National Honor Society; pursuing her BFA in English, creative writing through Southern New Hampshire University. Her sculpted poetry is often accompanied by her own multi-medium forms of art, photography, and spoken performance. The symbolic representation of inner dialog and fluid continuum of her thought processes is demonstrated by her signature use of italics and the tilde. Selections of her work have been translated into French, Italian, Spanish, Arabic, and German in a growing effort to foster cultural diversity and understanding through the voice of poetry. With over one hundred publishing credits, her work in all its mediums has been featured in a vast array of publications both in print and online. *Numinous* is her second book of poetry. A complete listing of her published works can be found at: www.leilafortier.com

ACKNOWLEDGEMENTS

Acoustic Ink: "Atonement," "Monsoon Emotion," "I Know Who You Are Now," "Offering," "Bhakti," "Silent Confession"

Damazine: "Veil"

Einstein's Pocket Watch: "Infinitely Testified," "Transparent," "Irreversible Devotion"

Full Armor Magazine: "You," "Living Prayer"

Gadfly: "Uncertain Eternity"

Gloom Cupboard: "Remains"

Guerilla Pamphlets: "Redeemed"

Indigo Rising Magazine: "Deeper Still," "Lacuna"

Knot Magazine: "Return to Eden," "Divine Apparition," "Diaphanous," "Saguna"

Liquid Imagination: "Swallowed"

Love is the Law: "Chrysalis," "Covet," "Virtuosity," "The Hidden Dimension," "Silent Equinox"

Magic Cat Press: "Fecund," "Apricot & Wheat"

Opium Poetry: "Fallen"

Outwardlink: "Dervish"

Parabola: "Refraction"

Pot Luck Magazine: "Absolve"

Red Lion Sq.: "Trip"

Sarasvati: "Monsoon Emotion," "Soul," "Opened"

Shuf Poetry: "Anointing Kiss"

Social-I: "Spaces In-Between"

The Electric Monsoon: "Numinous"

The Literary Yard: "Audible Secret," "Quickening"

The Mindful Word: "Synchro-Destiny," "Soul"

The Moronic Ox: "Delivered"

Torrid Literature: "Symmetry"

Trillium Literary Journal: "Monsoon Emotion," "Numinous"

Vagabondage Press: "Orchestra of Your Name"

Vox Poetica: "Love Is"

ZOUCH Magazine: "Delivered"

CPSIA information can be obtained at www.ICGtesting.com
Printed in the USA
LVOW01s0226311014

411290LV00004B/31/P